PREFACE

Non-ophthalmic trained medical practitioners and healthcare professionals demonstrate a high level of anxiety about the management of ophthalmic disease. Accurate diagnosis of ocular disease is important prior to treatment. A systematic approach to the examination of the eye is vital.

This book is designed to provide a simple guide to the differential diagnosis and management of common ophthalmic emergencies. The book is for all healthcare professionals who deal with patients with ophthalmic problems including Accident and Emergency doctors, General Practitioners, Optometrists, Orthoptists, Nurse Practitioners and Medical Students.

Don Gerard Rohan Jayamanne MBBS, FRCOphth
Consultant Ophthalmic Surgeon, United Kingdom

Photographic Contributions by:
Mr. A. Kostakis- Consultant Ophthalmic Surgeon, UK
Miss. A. Bhan- Consultant Ophthalmic Surgeon, UK
Miss. C. Ellerton-Consultant Ophthalmic Surgeon, UK
Mr. H. Harris- Ophthalmic Photographer

Acknowledgement to Mr Nick Exley for his expert help
A special thanks to Mr Ian Dawson

Email:firstcourse@fsmail.net
Address: Firstcourse-Medical LLP, PO Box 1123 , Doncaster England, DN1 9HQ.

Dedicated to JBJ and M&D

D1079197

CONTENTS

Page

The Painful Red Eye
Conjunctiva / Sclera

Cornea

Sudden Loss of Vision in a Quiet Eye

Neuro-ophthalmology

INTRODUCTION

Ophthalmic emergencies can be categorised into traumatic and non-traumatic, and further subdivided by considering whether the eye is painful, red or has reduced visual acuity. The red eye, although occasionally a feature of minor ocular disease, often indicates serious injury or disease. A rational and methodical examination of the eye will assist with differential diagnosis and aid management.

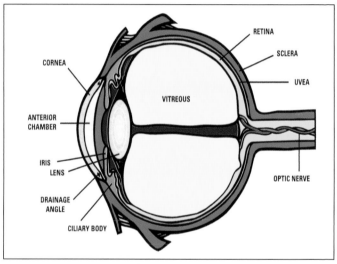

Figure 1. Simple anatomy of the eye
Vertical section through the eye

EXAMINATION

Visual acuity MUST always be recorded, one eye at a time, with the other eye occluded. This should be measured by reading a **Snellen chart** at a distance of **6 metres.** Patients must wear their distance glasses. However, if the glasses have been left at home or the patients are unable to read the 6/6 line accurately, a **pinhole vision** ought to be checked by placing a pinhole aperture in front of each eye. Children as young as 3 years of age may be able to cooperate with Snellen testing. Enquiry regarding **alterations in colour vision** should be documented in patients with suspected **traumatic or inflammatory optic nerve disease.**

Extraocular movements of the eyes in all fields of gaze should be examined in patients with trauma to the orbito-zygomatic region and in **all patients complaining of diplopia.** Anterior segment of the eye should be examined with a slit lamp or a magnifying loupe with a bright light source. Orientation of the eyelashes, appearance of the lid margins and presence of cysts on the lids should be noted. **Upper lid eversion** must be performed on all patients with a red, painful eye to inspect the palpebral conjunctiva.

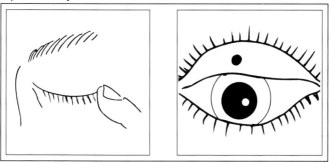

Figure 2. Technique of eyelid eversion
(Request the patient to look down, keeping their eyes open. Evert the lateral aspect of the upperlid using a cotton bud. Note: Subtarsal foreign body above)

Fluorescein should then be instilled. **A drop of local anaesthetic** may **aid examination** in a patient suffering from lid spasm. Conjunctival lacerations will appear yellow-green with a white light and bright green with a cobolt blue light.The normal cornea is smooth and clear.

The application of fluorescein to the tear film also detects the presence of corneal abrasions or foreign bodies. Abrasions will appear yellow-green with a white light and bright green with a cobalt blue light. Concentrated fluorescein dye applied over a potential site of corneal perforation will be diluted by the aqueous if a perforation and leak exist. A green stream will be visible within the dark orange dye. This sign is known as the **Siedel's test.**

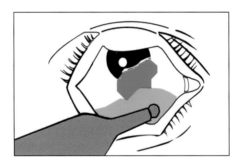

Figure 3. SIEDEL'S TEST TO DETECT A WOUND LEAK

Anterior chamber depth and clearness of the aqueous should be noted. The **accumulation of pus (hypopyon)** or **blood (hyphaema)** may be detected by shinning a bright light source if a slit lamp is absent. Colour and shape of the **Iris** should be noted. The pupils should be inspected for **size, shape and reaction** to direct and consensual light.

A rough determination of intraocular pressure may be made by palpation of the globe through closed lids. **Presence of a red reflex** should be noted and direct ophthalmoscopy performed to examine the **vitreous, optic nerve head and retina.** Visual field testing to confrontation will provide a rough estimate of the patient's visual field if a lesion is suspected in the visual pathway between the retina and occipital cortex.

DIFFERENTIAL DIAGNOSIS OF OCULAR SYMPTOMS

1.Transient loss of vision

Few minutes	Amaurosis fugax (TIA)	UNILATERAL
	Vertebrobasilar Insufficiency	BILATERAL
	Migraine	EITHER
	Impending retinal vein occlusion	UNILATERAL
	Ischaemic optic neuropathy	EITHER
	Giant cell arteritis	EITHER

2. Sudden, painless loss of vision

Central retinal artery or vein occlusion
Anterior ischaemic optic neuropathy
Vitreous haemorrhage
Retinal detachment

3. Sudden, painful loss of vision

Acute-angle closure glaucoma
Uveitis
Optic neuritis (associated with pain on eye movement)
Giant cell arteritis (associated with headaches)

4. Distortion of central vision

Acquired maculopathies

5. Double vision

Monocular
Spontaneous or traumatic dislocation/
subluxation of the lens

Binocular
Isolated third, fourth or sixth nerve palsies
Thyroid eye disease, Orbital mass
Internuclear ophthalmoplegia, Trauma
Myasthenia gravis

6. Flashing lights

Retinal hole/break or detachment,
posterior vitreous detachment, migraine

7. Floaters

Transient: Migraine
Constant: Posterior vitreous detachment,
uveitis, vitreous haemorrhage, retinal
detachment

8. Painless, red eye

Subconjunctival haemorrage, blepharitis,
dry eye syndrome

9. Painful, red eye

Mild	Conjunctivitis, episcleritis, foreign body
Moderate	Abrasions and corneal ulcers
Severe	Anterior uveitis, scleritis, acute-angle closure glaucoma

10. Foreign body sensation

Corneal abrasion or foreign body, dry eye
syndrome, blepharitis, conjunctivitis,
contact lens-related keratitis,
corneal ulcer, episcleritis

11. Itchiness and tearing

Allergic conjunctivitis, contact lens-related
problems, malposition of eyelashes,
nasolacrimal duct obstruction

12. Light sensitivity (photophobia)

Red eye: Anterior uveitis, corneal abrasion
Quiet eye: Migraine, meningitis, subarachnoid
haemorrhage (associated with headaches)

DIFFERENTIAL DIAGNOSIS OF OCULAR SIGNS

1. Eyelid swelling and erythema

Allergy (bilateral), periorbital cellulitis (unilateral), orbital cellulitis (unilateral), herpes zoster ophthalmicus (unilateral), hypothyroidism (bilateral)

2. Ptosis

Third nerve palsy, Horner's syndrome, myasthenia gravis, trauma, age-related, mechanical (mass on lid)

3. Proptosis

Thyroid eye disease, orbital cellulitis, orbital tumours, trauma, varix, orbital pseudotumour

4. Corneal oedema

Diffuse

Acute angle closure glaucoma and other causes of acute intraocular pressure elevation, congenital or acquired corneal dystrophies, surgical or non surgical trauma, contact lens overwear

Localised

Herpes simplex or zoster keratitis, microbial keratitis, contact lens keratitis, old corneal scar

5. Hyphaema

Trauma, spontaneous bleed from iris neovascularisation, blood dyscrasia or clotting disorder

6. Hypopyon
Microbial corneal ulcer, endophthalmitis following intraocular surgery, severe anterior uveitis

7. Vitreous opacities
Vitreous haemorrhage, asteroid hyalitis, posterior uveitis

8. Absent red reflex
Dense cataract, diffuse corneal oedema, vitreous haemorrhage, retinal detachment, severe intraocular inflammation (Retinoblastoma in a child)

9. Macular haemorrhage
Age-related macular degeneration, macular vein occlusion,diabetes, high myopia, traumatic choroidal rupture

10. Retinal haemorrhages
Diffuse

Central retinal vein occlusion, diabetic retinopathy, hypertensive retinopathy, hyperviscosity syndromes

Localised

Diabetic retinopathy, branch vein occlusion, hypertensive retinopathy, retinal macroaneurysms

11. Cotton wool spots
Diabetes, hypertension, systemic vasculitis, vein occlusion, arteriole occlusion, anaemia, leukaemia, HIV retinopathy

12. Macular exudates

Diabetes, hypertension, age related macular disease, vein occlusion, retinal macroaneurysms

13. Retinal new vessels

Diabetes, central or branch vein occlusion, chronic uveitis, rarely central retinal artery occlusion

14. Optic disc swelling

Papilloedema, papillitis, malignant hypertensive retinopathy, central retinal vein occlusion, ischaemic optic neuropathy, vasculitis, infiltration of the disc, pseudopapilloedema (disc drusen)

15. Optic disc pallor

Glaucoma, previous retinal artery or vein occlusion, post optic/retrobulbar neuritis, compression of optic nerve, traumatic optic neuropathy

16. Afferent pupil defect

Optic nerve disease, central retinal artery or vein occlusion, retinal detachment

17. Normal ocular examination with decreased vision

Amblyopia, retrobulbar neuritis, nutritional optic neuropathy, rare retinal dystrophies, functional visual loss, refractive errors

TRAUMA

Eyelid Lacerations

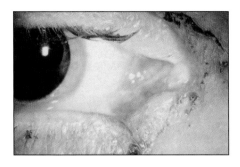

Injuries to the globe may be hidden and obscured by overt lid damage. Therefore, the eye should be carefully examined before eyelids are treated. Orbital fractures and embedded foreign bodies must always be considered. Radiographs may be needed to exclude these possibilites.

Management
Eyelid lacerations may be repaired even as long as 24 hours after the injury, due to it's rich vascular supply. Lacerations that cross the margin of the eyelid, involving the medial canthus, the lacrimal apparatus, levator complex of the upper eyelid or those associated with ocular trauma such as penetrating injuries should be referred directly to an ophthalmology department.

All other eyelid lacerations can be repaired with 6/0 synthetic monofilament sutures. Consider patients for tetanus prophylaxis.

Peri-Orbital Haematoma (Black Eye)

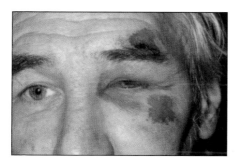

Usually caused by a direct blow to orbital region (eg. punch)

Management
Check visual acuity with pinhole aperature. Check for globe damage by examining the cornea for lacerations/abrasions, the anterior chamber for hyphaema and pupils for an afferent pupillary defect. Examine posterior pole for presence of a red reflex. Test the eye movements and palpate the bony margin of the orbit. If a bony injury is suspected perform facial radiographs. In the absence of significant ocular/orbital injury, prescribe topical eye ointment and analgesics and review within 36-48 hours.

Orbital Blow-out Fracture
Symptoms
Pain around orbit, pain on ocular movement, diplopia, tingling over the maxilla.
Signs
Restricted eye movement, bony tenderness, enophthalmos, surgical emphysema around the orbit (usually with associated medial wall blow-out fractures), tingling in the distribution of the infraorbital nerve.

Causes

Orbital blowout fractures commonly result from fist fights, contact sports and falls. The classical 'blow-out' is a fracture of the orbital floor without associated fracture of the orbital rim. The orbital blow-out fracture is characterised by depression of the floor of the orbit, often with herniation of orbital contents into the maxillary antrum. Patients may also have medial wall blowout fractures in addition to orbital floor fractures. Medial wall fractures may cause restricted or painful abduction and surgical emphysema around the orbit.

Management

Check visual acuity with pinhole aperture. Check for globe damage by examining the cornea for lacerations/abrasions, the anterior chamber for hyphaema and pupils for an afferent pupillary defect. Examine posterior pole for presence of a red reflex. Test eye movements. In the absence of significant ocular injury refer to a maxillo-facial department. Start broad spectrum antibiotics.

Conjunctival Lacerations

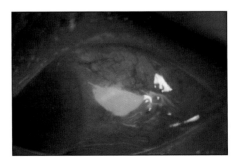

Symptoms

Foreign body sensation, tearing, mild discomfort, red eye.

Signs

Conjunctival haemorrhage, fluorescein staining of the conjunctiva.

Causes
Scratch from finger or foreign body.
Management
Complete ocular examination to exclude a ruptured globe. In the absence of any other significant ocular injury prescribe topical antibiotics. Even large lacerations (up to 1.5cm) heal without surgical repair. Topical non-steroidal anti-inflammatory drugs may offer effective pain relief. Review within one week.

Conjunctival/Subconjunctival Foreign Body

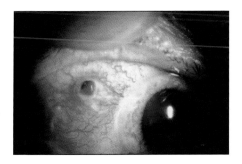

Symptoms
Foreign body sensation, discomfort, tearing, red eye.
Signs
Conjunctival haemorrhage, fluorescein staining of the conjunctiva and/or cornea. (Note: vertically orientated corneal staining pattern when a foreign body is under the upper eyelid).
Causes
Grit blowing into eye. Be wary when a history of hammering or grinding is present.
Management
Complete ocular examination to exclude a ruptured globe. Evert upper eyelid. In the absence of any other significant ocular injury remove object with a moistened cotton-wool bud after instilling local anaesthetic. Prescribe antibiotic ointment for a few days.

Corneal Foreign Body/Rust Ring

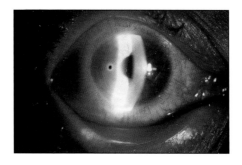

Symptoms
Foreign body sensation, tearing, photophobia, blurred vision.
Signs
Corneal foreign body (may be obvious or revealed by fluorescein), rust ring, red eye.
Causes
Grit blowing into eye, history of grinding or hammering.
Management
Complete ocular examination to exclude a ruptured globe. In the absence of any other significant ocular injury, instil local anaesthetic drops and attempt removal with moistened cotton-wool bud or 25-gauge needle introduced from the side. Once removal of the foreign body is complete, if a history of hammering is present obtain a X-ray to exclude an intraocular foreign body. Prescribe antibiotic ointment and review within 48 hours. A small amount of residual rust staining is acceptable. Over zealous debridment may lead to permanent scarring. Deep or stubborn foreign bodies on the visual axis or foreign bodies with extensive rust rings should be referred to an ophthalmology department.

Corneal Abrasion

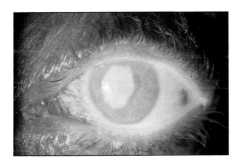

Symptoms
Foreign body sensation, tearing, photophobia, pain, red eye.
Signs
Corneal epithelial staining with fluorescein, diffuse conjunctival injection, blepharospasm.
Causes
Scratching of the eye with a finger, stick, leaf or piece of paper.
Management
Instil local anaesthetic drops to examine the eye. Evert upper eye-lid to make sure no subtarsal foreign body is present. Document size of abrasion. In the absence of any other significant ocular injury prescribe topical antibiotics. An eye pad may be of benefit. Topical and/or oral non-steroidal anti-inflammatory drugs may offer effective pain relief. Avoid prescribing local anaesthetics as these can delay healing. Review daily until the cornea has fully healed. If there is a delay in healing, worsening of symptoms or evidence of an infected corneal ulcer refer to an ophthalmology department.

Flashburn (Welder's Arc Eye)

Symptoms
Foreign body sensation, tearing, photophobia, red eye.

Signs
Punctate staining of the cornea with fluorescein, diffuse conjunctival injection, blepharospasm.

Causes
Exposure to ultraviolet light from welding or a sunlamp without using eye protection (goggles).

Management
Instil one drop of local anaesthetic prior to examination. Do not prescribe regular local anaesthetics as this can delay epithelial healing. Antibiotic ointment and eye pad. Regular oral analgesia. Condition usually settles within 24 hours.

Chemical Burns

Symptoms
Pain, stinging, grittiness, itchiness, photophobia, blurred vision, red eye.

Signs
Diffuse conjunctival injection, corneal epithelial staining with fluorescein, conjunctival chemosis, anterior chamber flare and cells, severe alkali burns (ammonia) may result in blanching of

perilimbal conjunctival vessels and corneal oedema and opacification with no view of the anterior chamber or iris.

Causes
Alkalis such as ammonia, lime, cement, bleach and acids such as battery acid. Alkali burns are more severe than acid burns due to rapid penetration of the cornea and anterior chamber resulting in disruption and damage of cells.

Management
Instil local anaesthetic drops to examine the eye. Immediate treatment is copious irrigation with either normal saline or water, for at least 30 minutes or until pH paper reveals readings that are close to neutral. Care must be taken to irrigate upper and lower fornices. Once irrigation is complete refer to an ophthalmology department for further advice and assessment.

Hyphaema

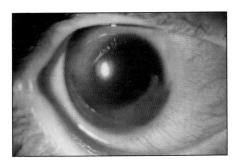

Symptoms
Mild to moderate visual disturbance or blurred vision, photophobia, tearing, red eye.

Signs
Blood in the anterior chamber which settles inferiorly to form a level, diffuse circumcorneal injection.

Causes
Direct blow to the eye by blunt trauma e.g. clenched fist or squash ball injuries.

Management
Immediate referral to ophthalmology department to exclude other contusional injuries to the anterior and posterior segments e.g. lens dislocation, choroidal rupture, retinal commotio.

Traumatic Optic Neuropathy

Symptoms
Decreased or blurred vision, loss of colour vision after a traumatic injury.

Signs
Afferent pupillary defect, loss of colour vision (subtle losses may be difficult to assess without formal colour vision testing methods), acutely the optic nerve will appear normal, signs of blunt trauma around the orbit e.g. bruising, swelling, bony tenderness.

Causes
Blunt trauma to the orbito-zygomatic region e.g. fist fights, falls, contact sports. Traumatic optic neuropathy is an optic nerve contusion or compression. Haematoma, ischaemia, or direct bone fragment penetration of the optic nerve may be the cause. Traumatic optic neuropathy is an impact injury to the optic nerve, the injury may be permanent or temporary. Visual loss is usually instantaneous. Typically patients with traumatic optic neuropathy have a visual acuity which is 6/60 or less. Window of opportunity for intervention in the treatment of intracanalicular optic nerve injuries may be less than eight hours.

Management
Immediate referral to an ophthalmology department for radiographic imaging of the optic nerve. Treatment with intravenous steroids or optic nerve sheath decompression may be indicated.

Ruptured Globe/Penetrating Ocular Injury

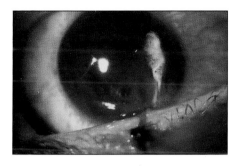

Symptoms
Severe pain, loss of vision.

Signs
Subconjunctival haemorrhage, full thickness scleral or corneal laceration, fluorescein testing reveals aqueous leak from corneal laceration (Siedel's test), shallow anterior chamber, hyphaema, irregular pupil, intraocular contents such as lens and vitreous may be outside of the globe, intraocular foreign body may be visible. (Note: Do not put pressure on the globe if perforation is suspected.)

Causes
History of high velocity injury e.g. hammering, windscreen injury.

Management
Tetanus prophylaxis, X-ray, plastic eye shield and urgent ophthalmology review.

CONDITIONS AFFECTING THE EYELIDS AND ORBITS

Orbital Cellulitis

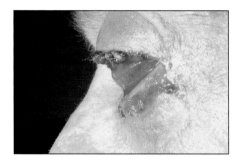

(Denotes the infection of tissues behind the orbital septum.)

Symptoms
Frontal headaches associated with fever and rigors, diplopia and loss of vision.

Signs
Lid swelling, proptosis, chemosis, limitation of ocular movements, abnormal pupil reactions, optic disc swelling and sinus tenderness.

Causes
The orbit is usually infected from a neighbouring structure; often sinusitis.

Management
Immediate referral to otolaryngology/ophthalmology department for investigation and treatment with high dose intravenous antibiotics. Life threatening condition.

Periorbital Cellulitis

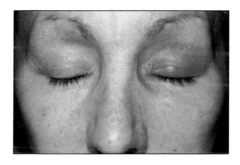

(Denotes the infection of tissues in front of the orbital septum).

Symptoms
Frontal ache, inability of eyelid opening, systemic symptoms including fever.

Signs
Facial cellulitis with gross swelling of eyelids with closure of the lids, eye retains full range of movement, it is not proptotic, and the visual acuity is unaffected.

Causes
Sinusitis in young children, cellulitis of the eyelids from an infected cyst (chalazion or stye).

Management
Immediate referral to otolaryngology if sinusitis is suspected in a young child. Like cellulitis elsewhere, parenteral antibiotics may be indicated.

Blepharitis

Symptoms
Burning, itching, foreign body sensation, crusting around the eyelids.

Signs
Lid margin may show telangiectatic blood vessels, a hard crust, ulceration and occasionally a waxy appearance. Punctate corneal staining with fluorescein.

Causes
Chronic Staphylococcal infection around the bases of the lashes. Frequently associated with dry eye syndrome and atopic eczema.

Management
Lid hygiene with scrubbing of the eyelid margins with mild baby shampoo, 2 week course of topical antibiotic ointment. A course of oral antibiotics for a few weeks may be helpful in severe cases. Topical treatment of associated atopic eczema. Artificial tears either drops or gels to restore the tear film in dry eye syndrome. Development of sensitivity to preservatives in artifical tears can be avoided by using a preservative free preparation.

Hordeolum (Stye)

Symptoms
Painful swelling on eyelid.

Signs
Tender inflamed swelling in the eyelid margin which points anteriorly through the skin.

Causes
Staphylococcal infection of a lash follicle.

Management
Most styes resolve spontaneously. Hot compresses and topical antibiotics. Surgical intervention rarely required.

Chalazion (Meibomian Cyst)

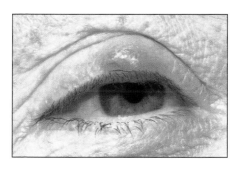

Symptoms
Painful or non-painful swelling on eyelid.
Signs
Tender or non-tender round, firm swelling arising from the tarsal plate.
Causes
Chronic inflammation of a meibomian gland.
Management
Topical antibiotics. On occasions chalazia disappear spontaneously. Some require incision and curettage. Routine referral to an ophthalmology department.

Trichiasis

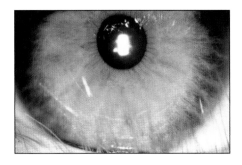

Symptoms
Grittiness, tearing, irritation.
Signs
Inward misdirection of eyelashes with contact of the lashes against the globe.
Causes
Blepharitis, chronic inflammation and entropion.
Management
Epilation of lashes as a temporary measure. Antibiotic or lubricant ointment. Referral to an ophthalmology department for cryotherapy/ electrolysis or surgery.

Entropion

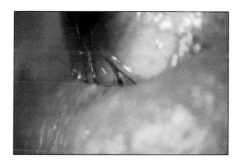

Symptoms
Red eye, tearing, foreign body sensation, grittiness.
Signs
Inward turning of the lid margin, inferior corneal, staining with fluorescein.
Causes
Aging, scarring of the conjunctiva secondary to chemical burns, trauma and ocular pemphigoid.
Management
Temporary measures include everting the eyelids with adhesive tape to prevent eyelashes touching the globe and antibiotic or lubricant ointment. Referral to an ophthalmology department.

Ectropion

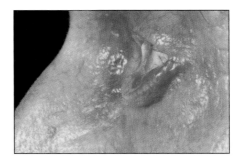

Symptoms
Ocular irritation, tearing, red eye.
Signs
Outward turning of eyelids, inferior corneal staining with fluorescein from exposure keratopathy.
Causes
Aging, seventh-nerve palsy, congenital.
Management
Treatment with ocular lubricants. Antibiotic ointment if secondary infection is present. Tape lids shut at night with adhesive tape. Referral to an ophthalmology department.

Dacryocystitis (Infection of the Lacrimal Sac)

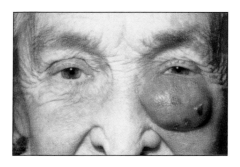

Symptoms
Swelling over the medial aspect of the lower eyelid, tearing, pain, fever; may be recurrent.

Signs
Localised, tender swelling over the nasal aspect of lower lid, purulent discharge when pressure applied over the lacrimal sac.

Causes
Nasolacrimal duct obstruction with secondary infection and inflammation of the lacrimal sac.

Management
Start systemic antibiotics after sending a swab for culture. Hot compresses. Refer patient to an ophthalmology clinic. Incision and drainage may be indicated.

Herpes Zoster Ophthalmicus

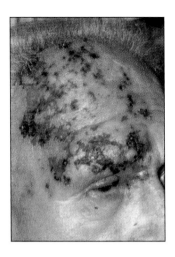

Symptoms
Rash, headache (pain and tingling often precede the rash), red eye, blurred vision, malaise.

Signs
Vesicular skin rash over the distribution of the ophthalmic division of the trigeminal nerve (does not cross the midline), conjunctival injection, staining of the cornea with fluorescein, localised or diffuse corneal oedema, anterior chamber flare and cells, cranial nerve palsies, optic nerve swelling.

Causes
Reactivation of Varicella-zoster virus in the sensory ganglion of the ophthalmic division of the trigeminal nerve.

Management
Treatment of the diverse ocular complications need specialist care. Refer the patient to an ophthalmology department. Patients with active skin lesions require oral anti-viral treatment.

THE PAINFUL RED EYE

CONJUNCTIVA AND SCLERA
Allergic Conjunctivitis

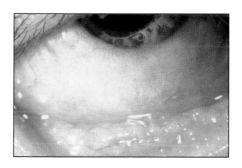

Symptoms
Itchiness, foreign body sensation, tearing, seasonal reactivation (usually bilateral).

Signs
Conjunctival injection, chemosis, eyelid oedema, signs of eczema on eyelids.

Causes
Atopy (allergy to pollens, dust etc), exposure to allergens causes sensitisation and subsequent contact results in inflammation associated with histamine release and mast cell degranulation.

Management
Removal of the offending allergen is not always possible. Treatment with antihistamines can offer immediate effective palliative relief from seasonal allergic conjunctivitis. Topical non-steroidal anti-inflammatory agents are alternatives. Mast cell stabilisers can be used and is prescribed as a prophylactic treatment. Refer to an ophthalmology department if no improvement as topical steroids are occasionally indicated.

Acute Microbial Conjunctivitis

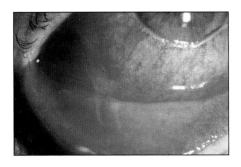

Symptoms
Grittiness, foreign body sensation, temporary blurring of vision cleared by blinking, discharge (mucous, purulent or watery), stickiness of eyelashes on waking.

Signs
Diffuse injection of the conjunctiva (including the tarsal conjunctiva) crusting on the eyelashes, punctate fluorescein staining of the cornea, preauricular lymphadenopathy.

Causes
Microbial conjunctivitis may be caused by infective agents such as bacteria and viruses. Symptoms and signs suggestive of infective conjunctivitis not responding to normal topical antibiotics may be caused by Chlamydial inclusion conjunctivitis.

Management
Treatment with topical antibiotics. Severe, recurrent or chronic conjunctivitis require referral to an ophthalmology department.

Ophthalmia Neonatorum
(Ocular infections acquired during the time the child is in contact with the mother's cervix and vaginal tract)

Symptoms
Purulent or mucopurulent discharge present from birth or a few days after birth, irritability.

Signs
Crusting on eyelashes, eyelid oedema, chemosis.
Causes
Bacterial (Gonococcal- purulent discharge within the first few days of life, Staphylococcal, Streptococcal), Chlamydial (conjunctivitis usually commences 5-12 days after birth), viral (Herpes simplex usually associated with vesicular rash), chemical (silver nitrate).
Management
Initial treatment depends on the result of the Gram's stain. Refer to an ophthalmology department.

Episcleritis

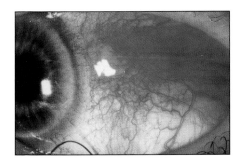

Symptoms
Ocular discomfort can be variable; painless or a dull ache may be present. Recurrent episodes of red eye.
Signs
Localised patchy sectorial redness, may take on the appearance of a nodule, dilated episcleral vessels run in a radial direction under the conjunctiva, vision normal.
Causes
Inflammation of the tissues between conjunctiva and sclera. Majority of cases are idiopathic; occasionally related to collagen vascular disease, gout and Herpes zoster.

Management
Mild episcleritis can resolve spontaneously but may recur. Moderate to severe episodes of episcleritis may require topical steroids and oral non-steroidal anti-inflammatory drugs and these patients should be referred to an eye department.

Scleritis

Symptoms
Blurred vision, severe and deep eye pain, headaches, photophobia, red eye.
Signs
Inflammation of the deep scleral vessels (large vessels that cannot be moved by brushing with a cotton wool bud), deep redness (sectorial or diffuse), sclera may appear bluish due to thinning with the underlying choroid visible, anterior chamber flare and cells, corneal oedema, proptosis, poor red reflex.
Causes
Autoimmune or granulomatous systemic diseases, previous Herpes zoster ophthalmicus.
Management
Immediate referral to an ophthalmology department for treatment.

Spontaneous Subconjunctival Haemorrhage

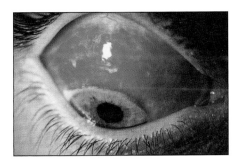

Symptoms
Sharp, stinging feeling; may be asymptomatic.
Signs
Diffuse or localised redness concealing the conjunctival vascular markings.
Causes
Spontaneous, precipitated by coughing or straining, recurrent episodes may be related with hypertension or blood dyscrasias.
Management
No treatment is required. Check blood pressure.

CORNEA

Microbial Keratitis

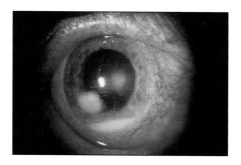

Symptoms
Acute red eye, discharge, ocular pain, photophobia, loss of vision.

Signs
Conjunctival injection, localised white opacity in the corneal stroma, mucopurulent discharge, corneal epithelial defect, hypopyon.

Causes
Infection of the cornea occurs after injury to the corneal epithelium (contact-lens wear, trauma or foreign body) or in immunocompromised hosts. Infective agents include bacteria, fungi or even acanthamoeba.

Management
Immediate referral to an ophthalmology department. Following corneal scrapings for cultures, commence intensive treatment with broad spectrum antibiotics until sensitivity reports are available.

Contact lens-related problems

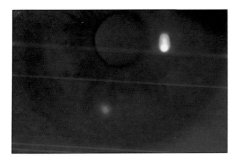

Symptoms
Pain, photophobia, red eye, mucopurulent discharge, grittiness.

Signs
Conjunctival injection, signs of microbial keratitis (see p36), mucous discharge, giant papilla on tarsal conjunctiva on lid eversion, punctate epithelial loss.

Causes
Microbial keratitis (see p36), hypersensitivity to preservatives, contact lens deposits, giant papillary conjunctivitis, poor lens fit, recurrent erosions.

Management
Microbial keratitis must always be ruled out in contact lens wearers with ocular pain and irritation (see p36). If doubt exists referral to an ophthalmology department is recommended. Conditions such as Giant papillary conjunctivitis can be treated with mast cell stabilisers. Patients with lens deposits or hypersensitivity to lens solutions must be referred to an optometry department.

Marginal Keratitis

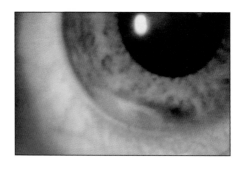

Symptoms
Mild irritation, eyelid crusting, foreign body sensation, epiphoria.

Signs
Red eye, marginal injection, mucopurulent discharge, blepharitis peripheral corneal curvilinear white opacities (infiltrates; single or multiple), minimal epithelial staining with fluorescein.

Causes
Hypersensitivity reaction to Staphylococcal blepharitis.

Management
Microbial keratitis must always be ruled out. Referral to an ophthalmology department is recommended. Eyelid hygiene and topical antibiotics in combination with mild steroids are the main treatment options. Steroid preparations should NOT be used without specialist advice.

Herpes Simplex Keratitis

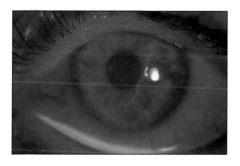

Symptoms
Recurrent episodes of red eye, photophobia, tearing, decreased vision, rash.

Signs
Vesicular rash, conjunctival injection, dendritic keratitis, localised corneal oedema, uveitis, preauricular lymph-adenopathy.

Causes
Herpes simplex virus infection.

Management
Corneal epithelial disease can be treated with topical anti-viral agents. Referral to an ophthalmology department is recommended.

Exposure Keratopathy

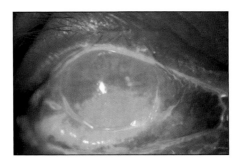

Symptoms
Irritation and foreign body sensation, dryness, burning. Symptoms usually worse on waking.

Signs
Poor blinking on the affected side, fluorescein staining on the lower one third of the cornea.

Causes
Seventh cranial nerve palsy (Bell's palsy), proptosis, eyelid deformity from trauma.

Management
Artificial tears or lubricant eye ointment. Lid taping or patching at night. Treat any secondary infection if present with antibiotics. Referral to an ophthalmology department to prevent progressive corneal damage. Surgical correction may be indicated.

Acute Glaucoma

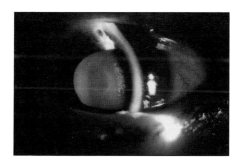

Symptoms
Intense pain, red eye, severe visual loss, coloured haloes around lights, headaches, nausea and vomiting.

Signs
Circumcorneal injection (blood vessel dilatation concentrated around the rim of the cornea), corneal oedema (loss of corneal transparency), shallow anterior chamber, mid-dilated and fixed pupil, stony-hard eye to palpation.

Causes
Patients with shallow anterior chambers (often hypermetropes), lens induced (phacomorphic), topical mydriatics in at risk eyes, previous ocular inflammation, drainage angle abnormalities.

Management
Immediate referral to an ophthalmology department for reduction of intraocular pressure.

Acute Anterior Uveitis (Iritis)

Symptoms
Deep ache in the eye, blurred vision, photophobia, red eye.
Signs
Circumcorneal injection (blood vessel dilatation concentrated around the rim of the cornea), anterior chamber hazy appearance (due to flare and cells), hypopyon may be present (collection of white blood cells), deposits on the cornea (keratic precipitates KP's), pupil may be small and irregular, eye may be hard on palpation if secondary glaucoma has developed.
Causes
HLA B27 related diseases, inflammatory bowel disease, post-viral (Herpes simplex/zoster), sarcoidosis, post-trauma, post-operative, idiopathic.
Management
Urgent referral to an ophthalmology department for treatment.

Central Retinal Artery Occlusion

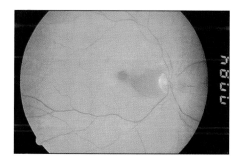

Symptoms
Unilateral acute painless loss of vision; may have a history of amaurosis fugax.

Signs
Whitening of the retina with a cherry-red spot in the center of the macula. An afferent pupil defect; poor visual acuity.

Causes
Emboli arising from the major arteries from the head/neck and from the left side of the heart. The emboli may be fatty deposits from atheromatous plaques, platelet thrombi or calcium deposits from heart valves. Giant cell arteritis must also be excluded.

Management
Retinal artery occlusion is an ophthalmic emergency and prompt treatment is essential. Immediate ocular massage and referral to an ophthalmology department. Surgical or medical lowering of intraocular pressure may improve outcome.

Central Retinal Vein Occlusion

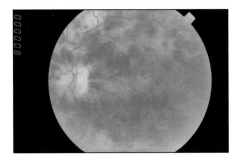

Symptoms
Unilateral painless loss of vision, transient visual obscurations may precede the visual loss.

Signs
Clinical appearances depend on the severity of the venous occlusion. Mild occlusions may result in minimal loss of vision and dilation of veins with occasional haemorrhages. Moderate to severe occlusions may result in gross reduction of vision, diffuse retinal haemorrhages in all quadrants of the retina, grossly dilated vessels, cotton wool spots and an afferent pupil defect.

Causes
Atherosclerosis of the adjacent retinal artery, hypertension, diabetes, hyperlipidaemia, glaucoma and hyperviscosity states.

Management
An early referral to an ophthalmology department is recommended. Cardiovascular assessment is recommended. There is no proven early treatment that will alter the visual prognosis in established central retinal vein occlusion (CRVO). However, patients with underlying medical disorders require treatment. Photocoagulation in eyes with an ischaemic vein occlusion can reduce risk of neovascular complications. Lowering of intraocular pressure in glaucoma patients is essential. Trials of intravitreal therapies for CRVO are ongoing.

Vitreous Haemorrhage

Symptoms

Sudden painless loss of vision associated with appearance of black spots or floaters, occasionally a shadow with flashing lights.

Signs

Absent red reflex, poor fundal view on ophthalmoscopy if severe, mild vitreous haemorrhage may only obscure inferior retinal details.

Causes

Diabetic retinopathy (usually a known history of diabetes), posterior vitreous detachment, retinal break, retinal detachment, previous retinal vein occlusion, macular degeneration.

Management

Immediate referral to an ophthalmology department is recommended. Ultrasound investigation of the posterior pole may identify treatable causes.

Retinal Detachment (Rhegmatogenous)

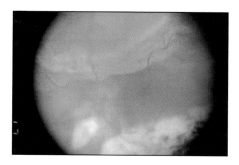

Fluid from the vitreous cavity collects in the potential space between the sensory retina and the retinal pigment epithelium through a retinal hole or tear.

Symptoms
Flashing lights, floaters or both, a shadow or curtain over the field of vision.

Signs
Visual field defect, loss of the red reflex, elevation of the retina, visible flap or break in the retina, an afferent pupil defect may be present, floppy mobile retina which moves with eye motion.

Causes
High myopia, trauma, previous intraocular surgery, complication of posterior vitreous detachment.

Management
Patients with an acute rhegmatogenous retinal detachment must be referred to an ophthalmology department so that surgical repair can be performed.

Age related Macular Degeneration (AMD)

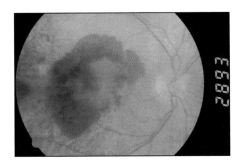

Dry form of AMD presents with gradual loss of central vision and is unlikely to present as an ocular emergency. Exudative or wet form of AMD is more likely to present with sudden loss of central vision.

Symptoms
Central scotoma, distortion of straight lines, reduction in vision, objects may appear altered in size and shape.

Signs
Central scotoma looking at print or distortion on Amsler chart testing, macular or paramacular retinal/subretinal haemorrhages, drusen (colloid bodies) at the posterior pole (also in fellow eye), pigmentation of the posterior pole.

Causes
Age related changes, soft drusen, hereditary, myopia.

Management
Immediate referral to an ophthalmology department for evaluation. In certain forms of AMD known as wet AMD, without treatment, vision loss may be sudden, severe and irreversible. This form of AMD is characterised by the development of abnormal blood vessels. A new treatment for wet AMD involves intravitreal injections of a drug which is an antibody fragment that inhibits vascular endothelial growth factor (VEGF) activity. Published results of studies on the treatment of wet AMD have shown that the benefits of the treatment includes maintenance of baseline vision whilst on anti-VEGF treatment in a majority of patients. About one third of patients on anti-VEGF treatment were shown to gain vision with the effect been sustained over the treatment period.

Posterior Uveitis
Symptoms
Floaters, blurred vision, occasionally photophobia

Signs
Vitreous debris, retinal exudates or infiltrates, retinal vasculitis, optic disc swelling, areas of scarring and pigmentation on the retina from previous episodes of inflammation.

Causes
Toxoplasmosis, sarcoidosis, pars planitis, viral (Herpes simplex, Varicella-zoster, Cytomegalovirus), Candida, Toxocariasis, Behcet's disease

Management
Immediate referral to an ophthalmology department for investigations. Treatment according to investigation findings.

ANTERIOR ISCHAEMIC OPTIC NEUROPATHY (AION)

Arteritic AION (due to underlying giant cell arteritis)

Symptoms
Initially unilateral sudden loss of vision in a white eye. Temporal headaches associated with jaw claudication, weight loss, loss of appetite, malaise, muscle pain, visual obscurations (fleeting episodes of visual loss lasting a few seconds) preceding visual loss.

Signs
Scalp tenderness, non-pulsatile superficial temporal vessels, optic disc swelling (can involve a sector of the disc), afferent pupillary defect.

Causes
Giant cell arteritis.

Management
Immediate referral to an ophthalmology department. Delay can cause permanent bilateral blindness. High dose corticosteroids should be given immediately.

Non-arteritic AION

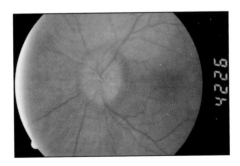

Symptoms
Sudden painless loss of vision (may complain of inferior hemi-field loss).

Signs
Afferent pupillary defect, optic disc swelling (can involve a sector of the disc), disc haemorrhages.

Causes
Arteriosclerosis, diabetes, hypertension, hypercholesterolaemia.
Management
Immediate referral to an ophthalmology department to exclude arteritic AION.

Optic/Retrobulbar Neuritis

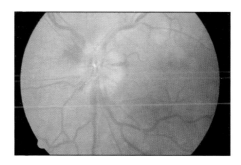

Retrobulbar neuritis refers to inflammation of the nerve that shows no abnormality on fundal examination.

Symptoms
Loss of vision over a few days (usually unilateral), loss of colour vision, reduced light intensity, visual symptoms may worsen when body temperature increases, pain on ocular movement, sensory or motor symptoms.

Signs
Afferent pupillary defect, decreased colour vision, central or centrocecal scotoma, optic disc swelling (normal disc in retrobulbar neuritis), retinal vasculitis.

Causes
Post-viral (measles, mumps, chicken pox etc), multiple sclerosis, post-vaccinations, idiopathic.

Management
Complete neurological examination and referral to a neurology department if focal neurological signs are identified for further investigation. Ophthalmology assessment is also indicated.

NEURO-OPHTHALMOLOGY

Diplopia
Sudden onset diplopia (double vision) can indicate palsies of the third, fourth and sixth cranial nerves. In all patients who complain of double vision, it is important to exclude palsies of these three nerves. Since ocular signs may be the initial pointer of significant neurological disease, complete physical assessment including cardiovascular and central nervous system examination should be carried out.

Third nerve palsy
Symptoms
Drooping eyelid, diplopia (unless complete ptosis is present), headache around the distribution of the ophthalmic branch of the trigeminal nerve.
Signs
Partial or complete ptosis, limitation of ocular movement in all directions of gaze except abduction (if the superior branch of the nerve is involved without inferior branch involvement, ptosis and limitation of elevation would be noted. However, if the inferior branch is paralysed with sparing of the superior branch, limitation of depression and adduction would be noted with pupil dilation), the eye displaced down and outwards. Pupil may be fixed, dilated, minimally reactive or normal.
Causes
Pupil involvement and presence of pain mean that an intracranial aneurysm or a compressive lesion in the cavernous sinus must be excluded immediately. Head trauma, microvasular disease, rarely cranial arteritis.
Management
Urgent referral to a neurosurgical department if pupil involvement is present. Pupil sparing third nerve palsies may be secondary to microvascular disease (typically diabetes, hypertension, hypercholesterolaemia), however referral to a neurology/ ophthalmology department is recommended.

Fourth nerve palsy

Symptoms
Binocular vertical/diagonal/tilted diplopia (disappears when one eye is occluded) worse when looking down to read, sensation that objects are tilted.

Signs
Head tilt to one side (usually opposite side to the superior oblique paresis), limitation of depression of the eye when looking down and in, affected eye appears higher in the primary position.

Causes
Closed head trauma, microvascular disease (typically diabetes, hypertension, hypercholesterolaemia), demyelinating disease, rarely tumours/aneurysms and cranial arteritis.

Management
Neurological/medical and ophthalmological assessment should be requested.

Six nerve palsy

Symptoms
Binocular horizontal diplopia (images side by side), diplopia worse for distance, sudden onset convergent squint.

Signs
Limitation of abduction of the affected eye.

Causes
Multiple causes because of the long intracranial course of the nerve, microvascular disease most common in older adults (diabetes, hypertension, hypercholesterolaemia), trauma, increased intracranial pressure, cavernous sinus mass, demyelinating disease, stroke (rare without other signs), rarely cranial arteritis.

Management
Neurological/medical and/or ophthalmological assessment should be requested.

Anisocoria (Pupils unequal in size)

The abnormal pupil is the one which is dilated

Causes

Previous blunt trauma with damage to the iris sphincter, Adie's tonic pupil, pharmacological dilation, Third nerve palsy (associated with ptosis and/or extraocular muscle paresis).

The abnormal pupil is the one which is constricted

Causes

Horner's syndrome (associated with mild ptosis, apparent enophthalmos, decreased sweating over the side of the face), acute iritis, Argyll Robertson pupil.

Management

Patients with suspected neurological causes of anisocoria such as sudden onset third nerve palsy and Horner's syndrome need to be investigated. Immediate neurological assessment should be requested.

Amaurosis Fugax

Symptoms

Monocular visual loss, lasts few seconds to minutes, occasionally a few hours. Vision usually returns to normal.

Signs

Ocular examination usually normal. Occasionally may see an embolus within the retinal arterial circulation.

Causes

Emboli from the carotid artery, heart or aorta. Emboli secondary to cardiac arrhythmia; hyperviscosity states.

Management

Conditions such as Giant cell arteritis, papilloedema and migraine can produce transient visual loss. Patients with monocular visual loss require careful ocular examination and medical examination (cardiac and carotid auscultation) and prompt referral to an ophthalmology department.

HEADACHES AND THE EYE

Most patients with a history of headaches around the eye do not have serious disease. However, headaches associated with visual symptoms can occasionally indicate life or sight threatening disease.

Symptoms and signs of serious disease

Giant cell arteritis

Symptoms
Temporal headaches associated with jaw claudication, weight loss, loss of appetite, malaise, muscle pain, sudden loss of vision or visual obscurations (fleeting episodes of visual loss lasting a few seconds).
Signs
Scalp tenderness, non-pulsatile superficial temporal vessels, ischaemic optic neuropathy (optic disc swelling), afferent pupillary defect.
Management
Immediate referral to an ophthalmology department. Delay can cause permanent bilateral blindness.

Episodes of angle closure glaucoma

Symptoms
Episodes of headaches associated with a red and painful eye, decreased vision, coloured haloes around lights, nausea and vomiting. Episodes are more likely to occur when the patients are in dimly lit rooms.
Signs
Blood vessel dilation concentrated around the corneal limbus, cloudy cornea, fixed mid-dilated pupil, shallow anterior chamber.
Management
Immediate referral to an ophthalmology department.

Orbital cellulitis from sinus disease

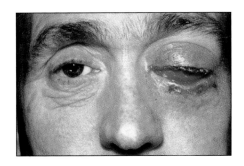

Symptoms
Frontal headaches associated with fever and rigors, diplopia and loss of vision.
Signs
Lid swelling, proptosis, chemosis, limitation of ocular movements, abnormal pupil reactions, optic disc swelling.
Management
Immediate referral to otolaryngology/ophthalmology department for investigation and treatment with high dose intravenous antibiotics. Life threatening condition.

Intracranial Space occupying lesion
Symptoms
Severe headaches (worse on waking in the morning and aggravated by coughing and straining), nausea, vomiting, transient visual obscurations, diplopia, generalised neurological symptoms such as poor coordination, unsteadiness.
Signs
Papilloedema, restriction of abduction (unilateral or bilateral sixth nerve palsy), visual field loss.
Management
The patient requires immediate assessment by a neurology department.

Malignant Hypertension
Symptoms
Severe headaches typically located in the occipital region, blurred vision or transient visual obscurations.
Signs
Retinal cotton wool spots, haemorrhages, optic disc swelling and elevated blood pressure.
Management
Immediate admission to hospital and medical treatment.

Cluster headaches
Symptoms
Unilateral periorbital, frontal headache associated with tearing, rhinorrhea, sweating and ptosis. Typically cyclic (once or twice daily for two weeks).
Signs
Ipsilateral conjunctival injection, ptosis, Horner's syndrome.
Management
Referral to a neurology department to exclude more serious pathology.

Migraine

Symptoms

Unilateral or bilateral headaches associated with nausea and vomiting, photophobia, visual disturbances such as zig-zag lines and fortification scotoma. Blurred vision, obscuration of vision or visual field loss lasting up 60 minutes. Additional neurological symptoms (motor or sensory).

Signs

Pupillary abnormalities and ocular motility problems may be present. Usually none.

Management

Referral to a neurology department for investigation and treatment.

Headaches associated with a third nerve palsy
Posterior communicating artery aneurysm

Symptoms

Headaches and pain around the eye, diplopia, blurring of vision, photophobia, neck stiffness, abnormal behaviour, neurological symptoms.

Signs

Complete or partial ptosis on the side of the headache, restricted eye movements, dilated pupil, altered mental state, rarely sub-hyaloid haemorrhage.

Management

Immediate referral to a neurosurgical department.

Note: Subarachnoid haemorrhage from a posterior communicating artery can give rise to a dense vitreous haemorrhage.